scribble page.

NOT JUST A COLORING BOOK

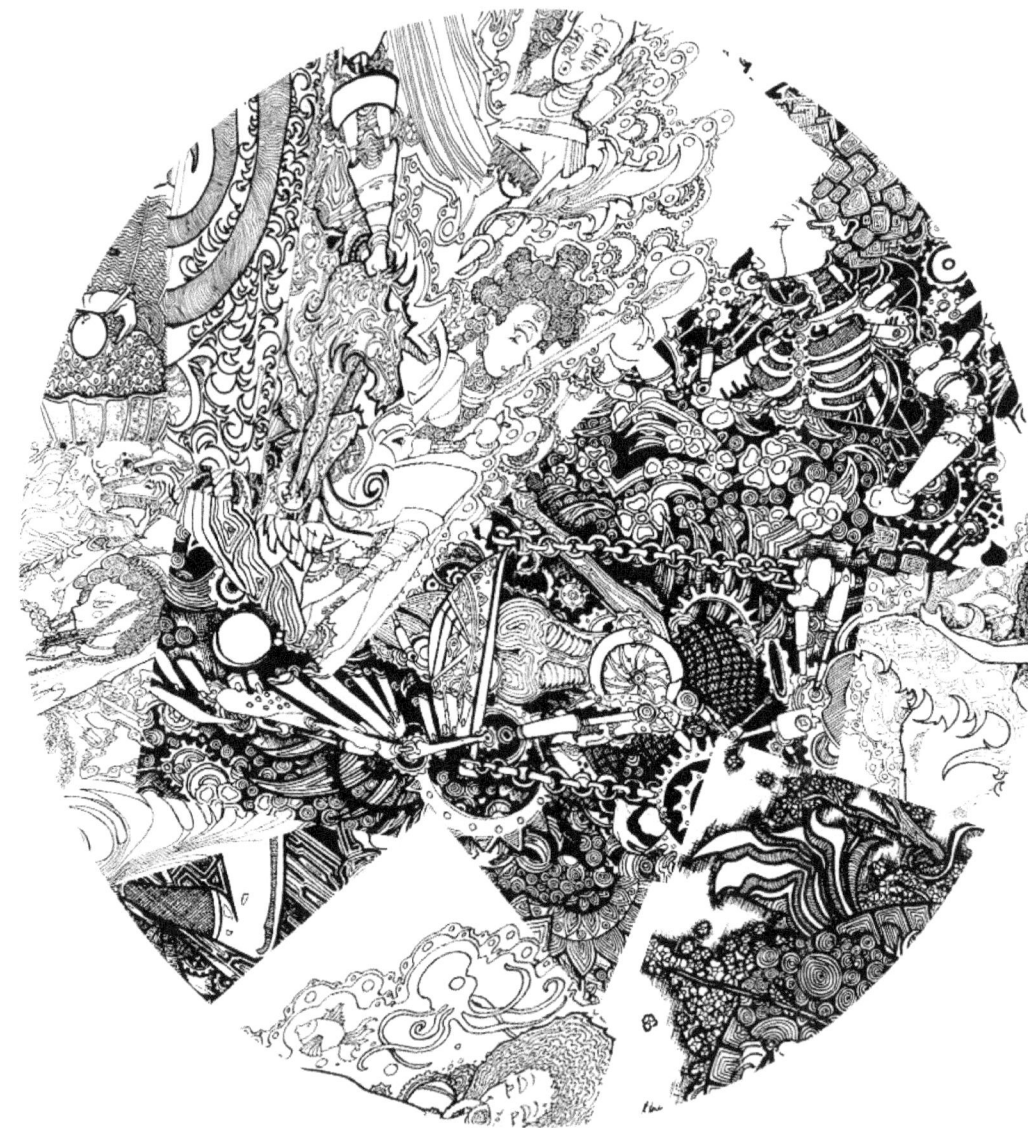

I look at this book
more like a collaboration
between You and I. So empty
your mind of troubles and calm
thou heart this next step is yours
and I have faith in you!

scribble page.

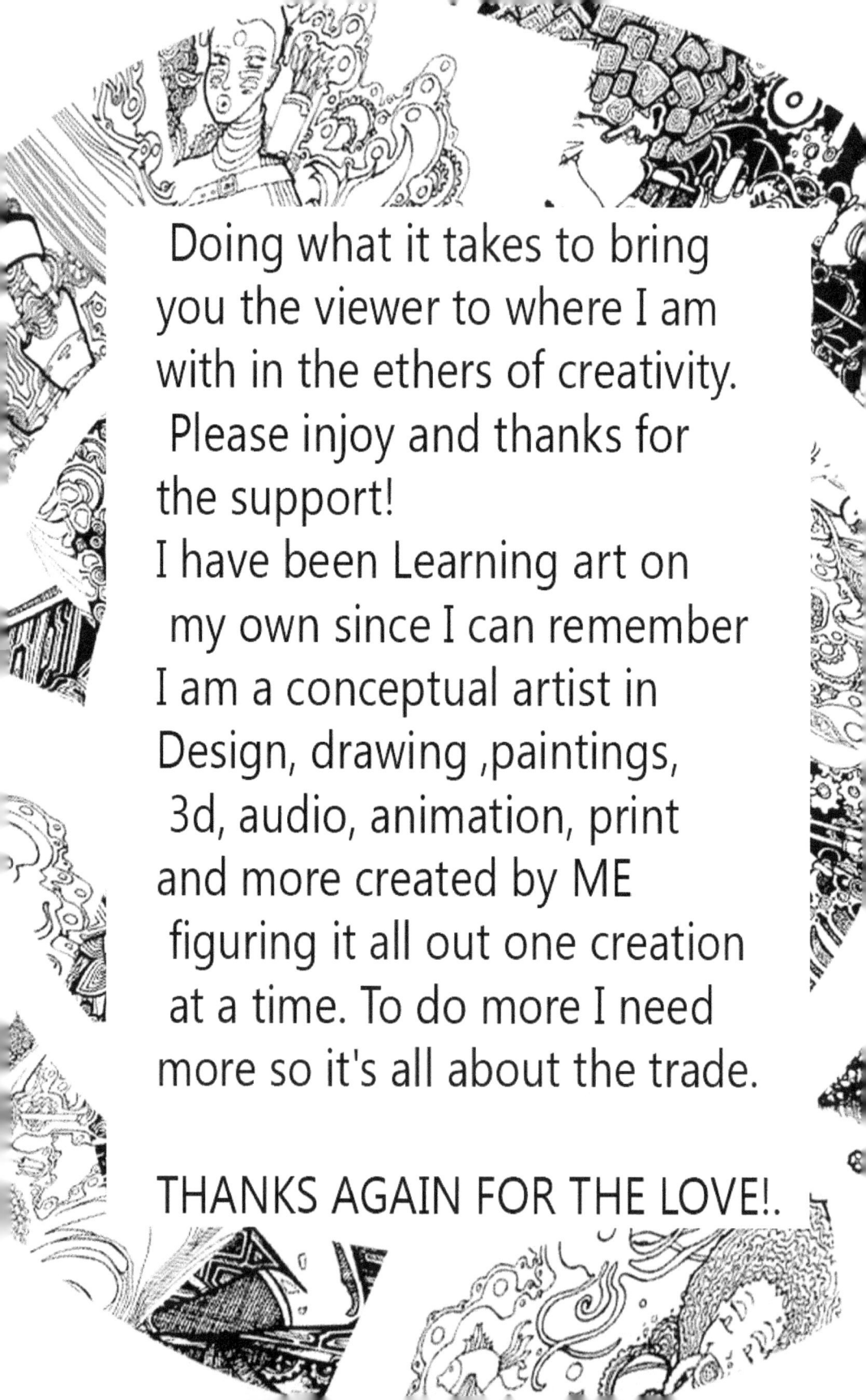

Doing what it takes to bring you the viewer to where I am with in the ethers of creativity. Please injoy and thanks for the support!
I have been Learning art on my own since I can remember I am a conceptual artist in Design, drawing ,paintings, 3d, audio, animation, print and more created by ME figuring it all out one creation at a time. To do more I need more so it's all about the trade.

THANKS AGAIN FOR THE LOVE!.

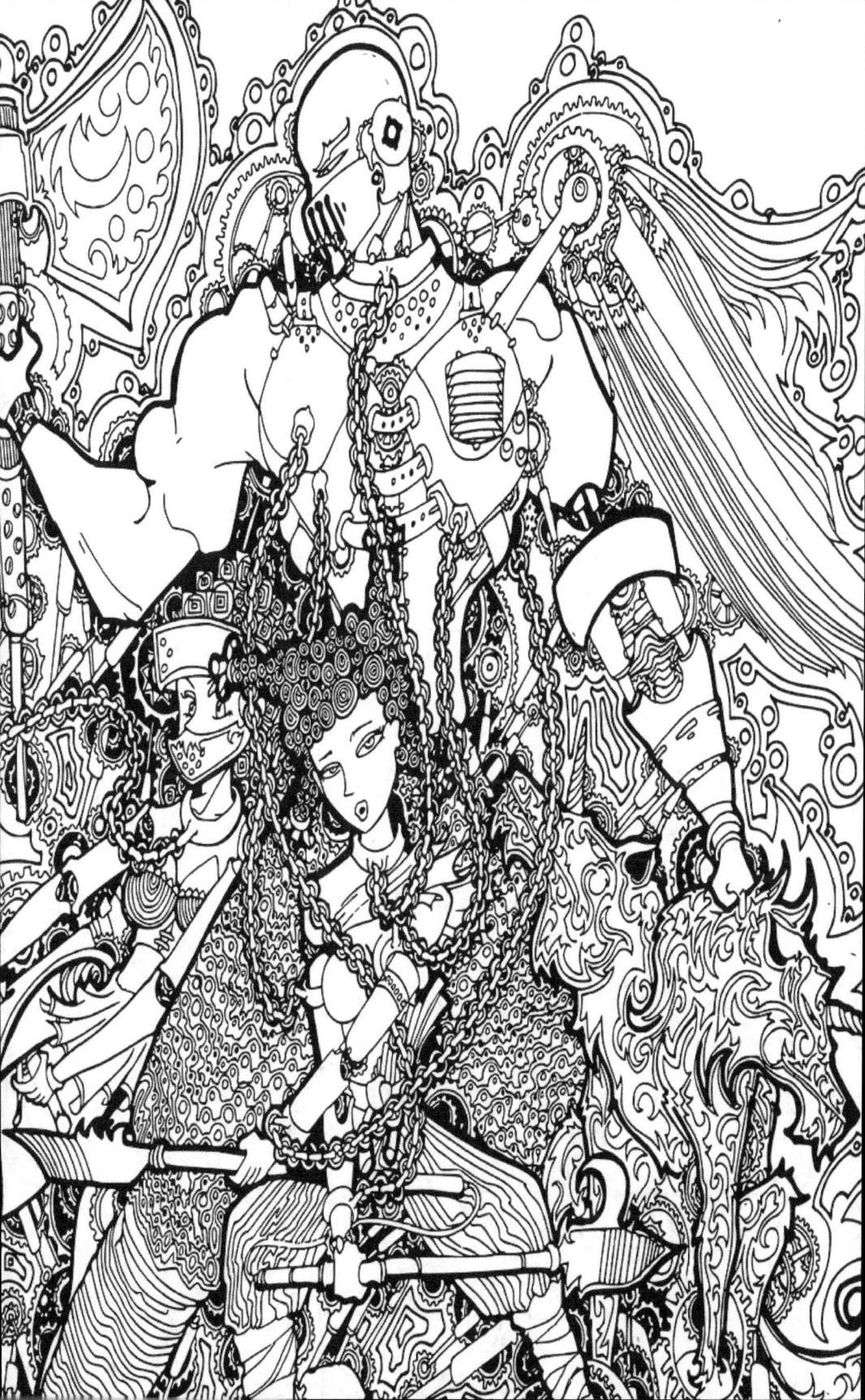

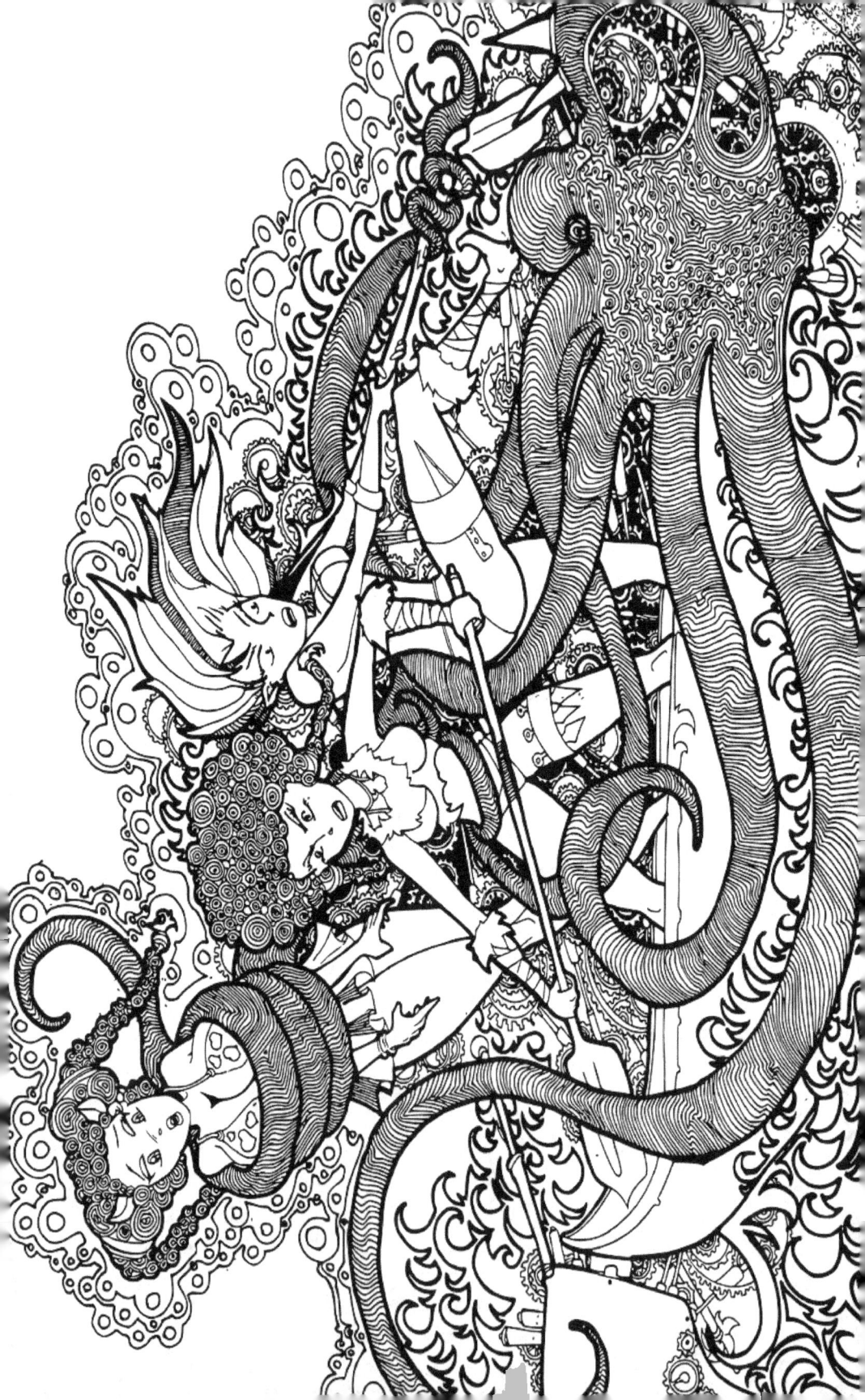

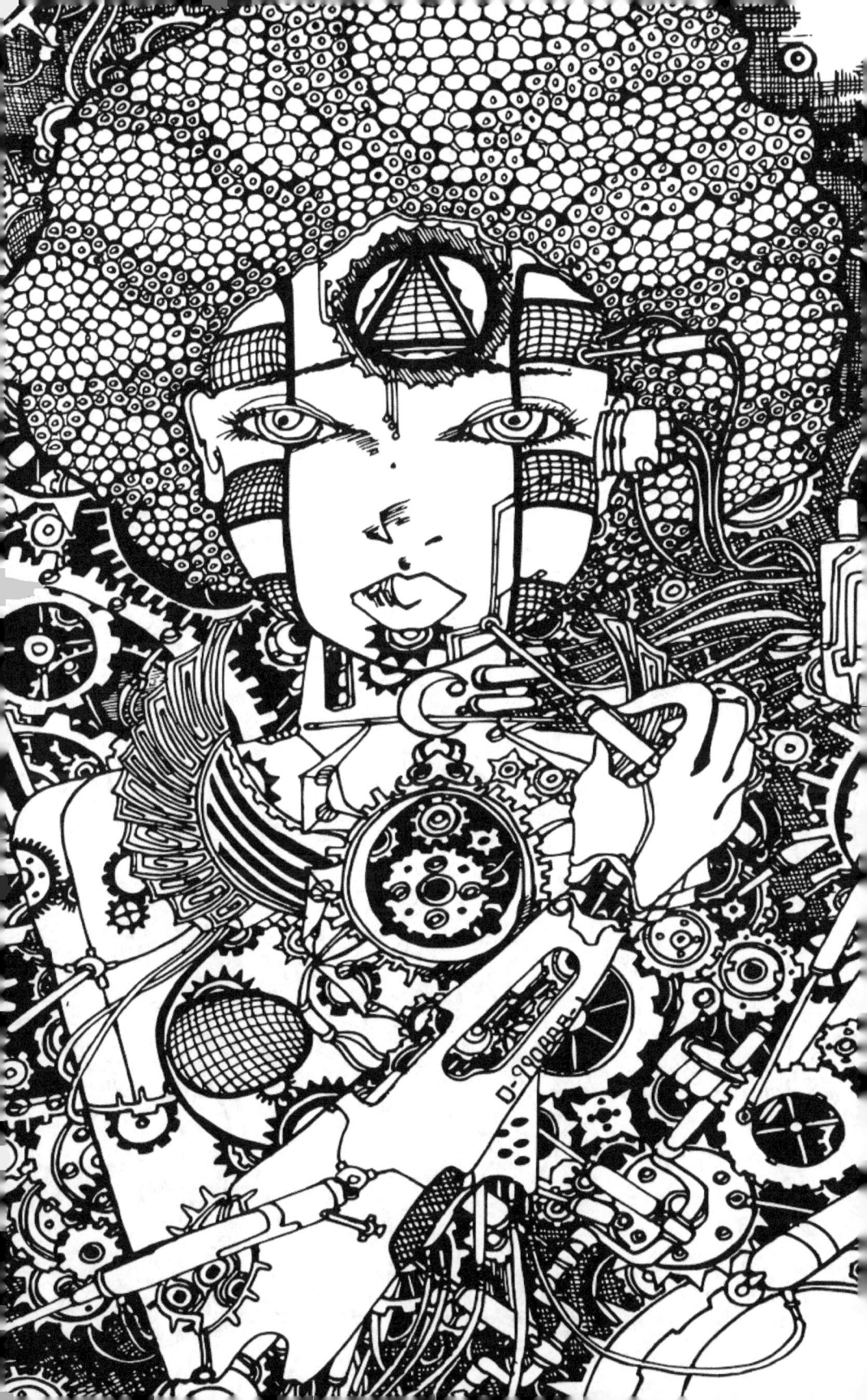

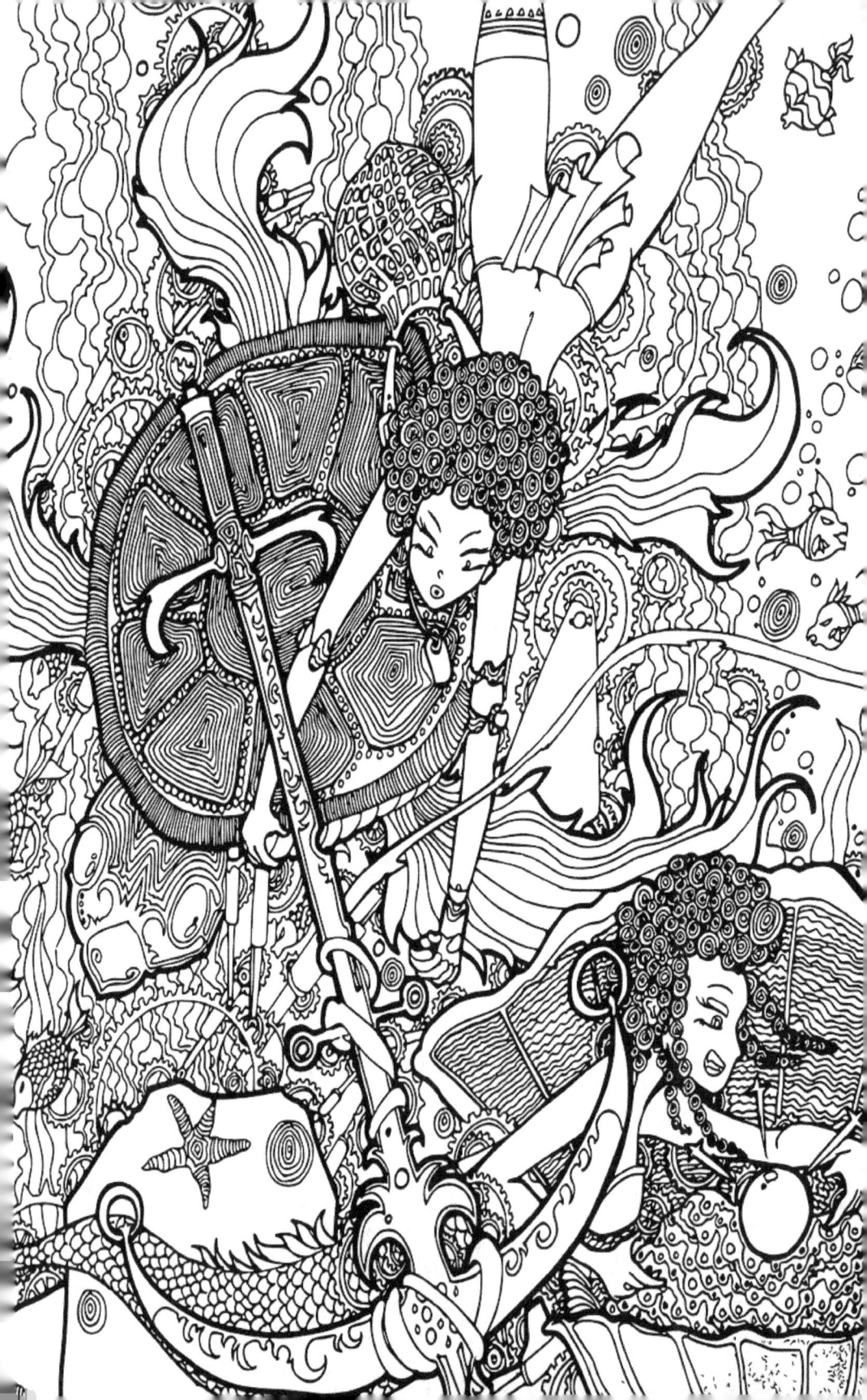

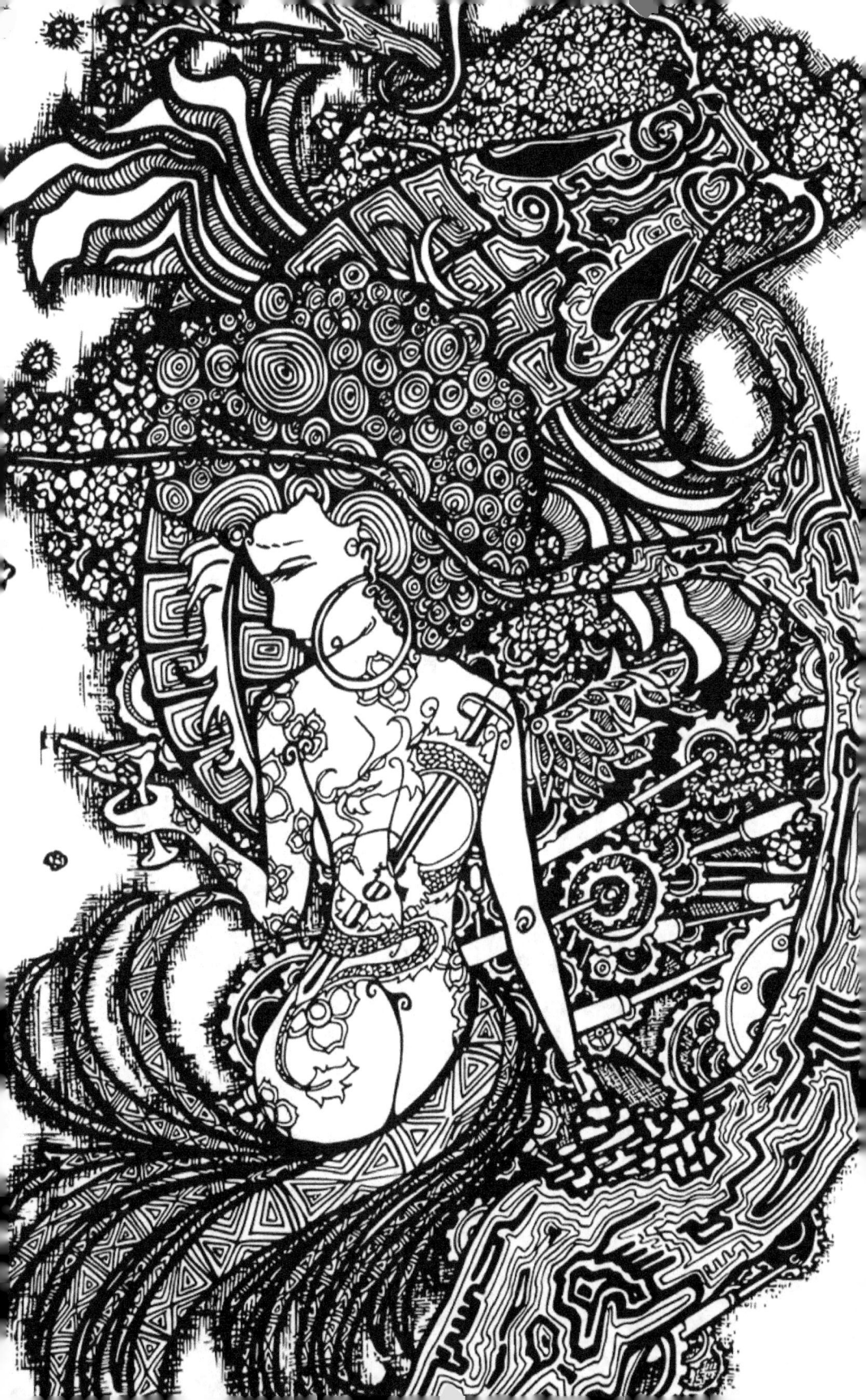

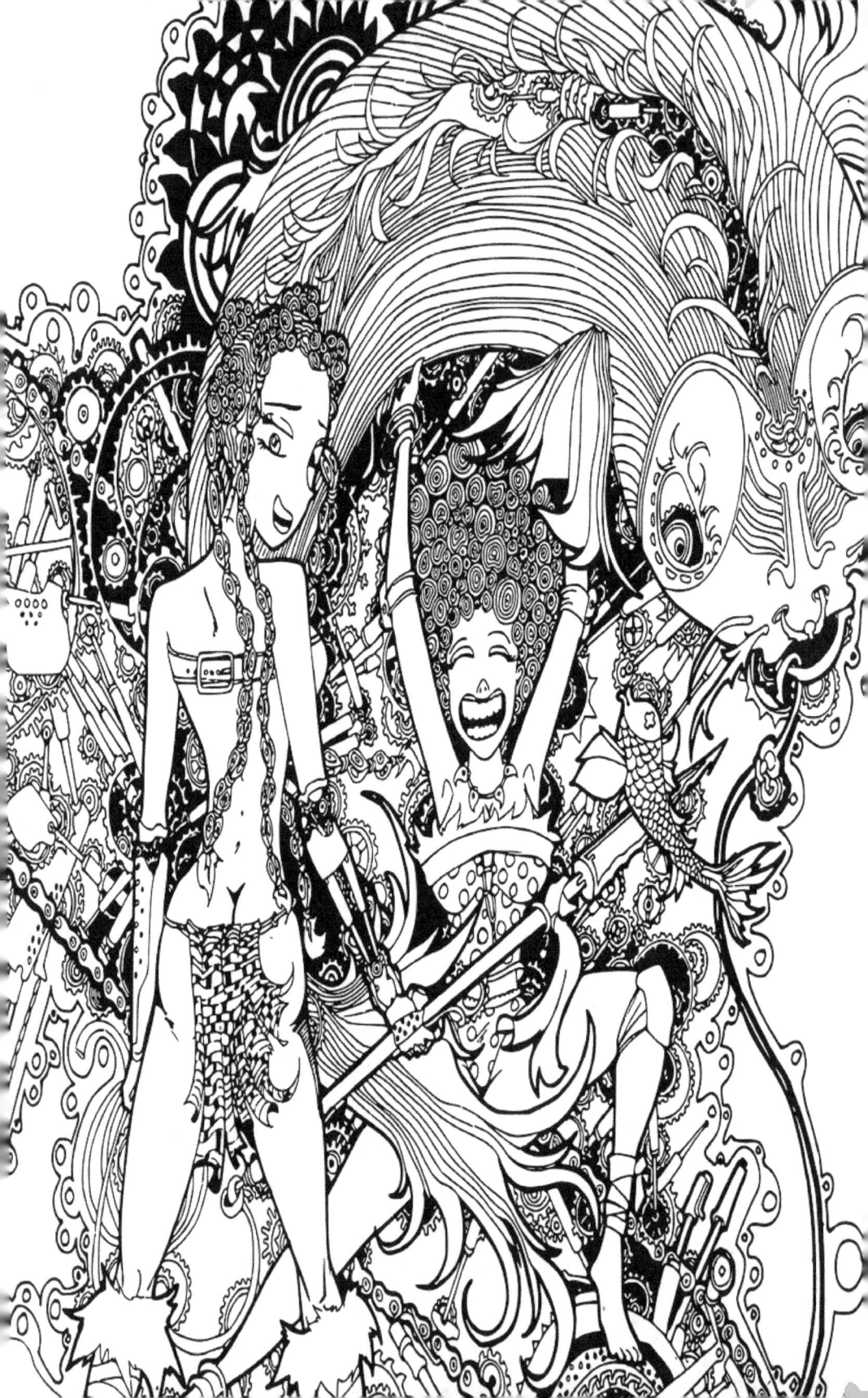

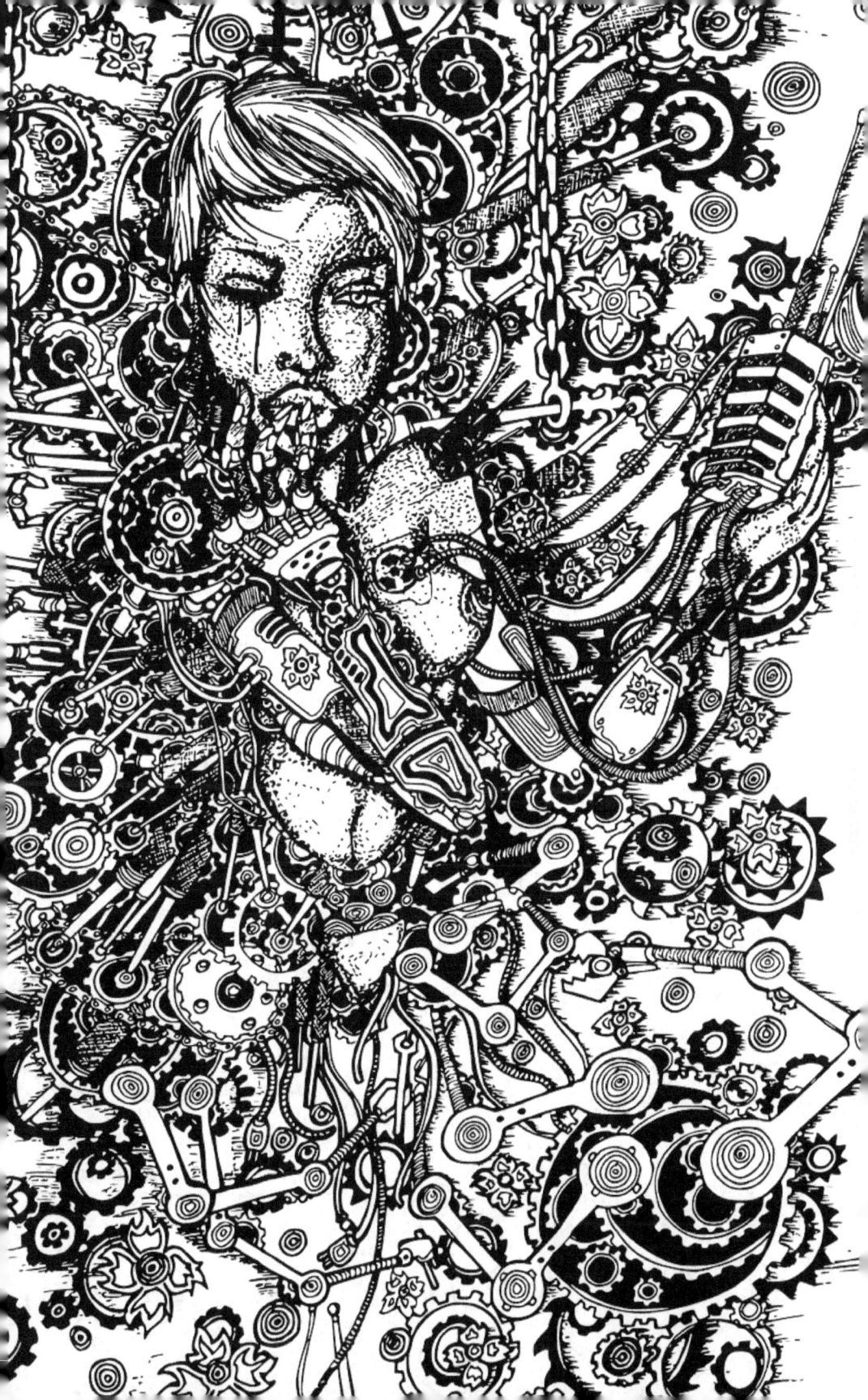

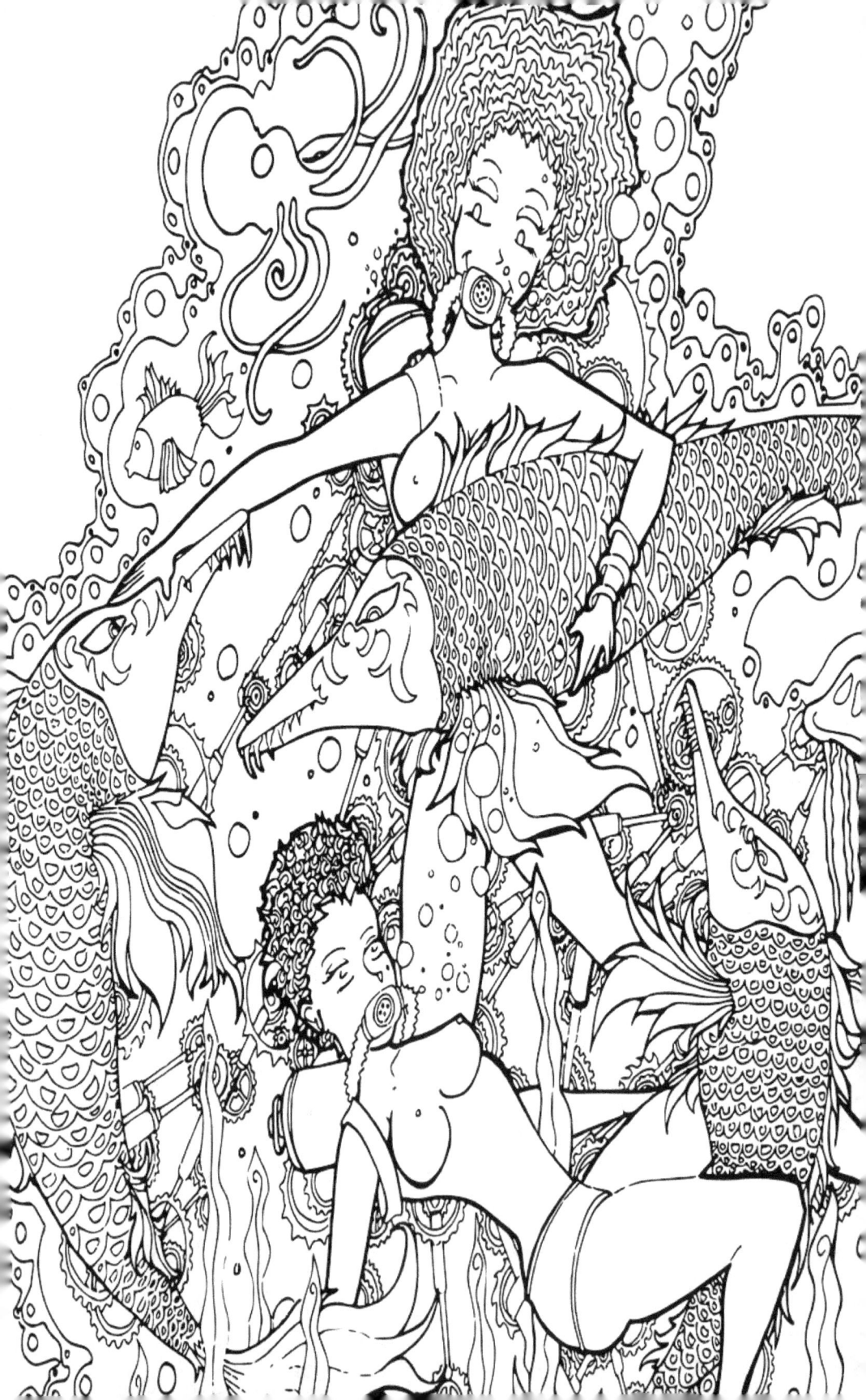

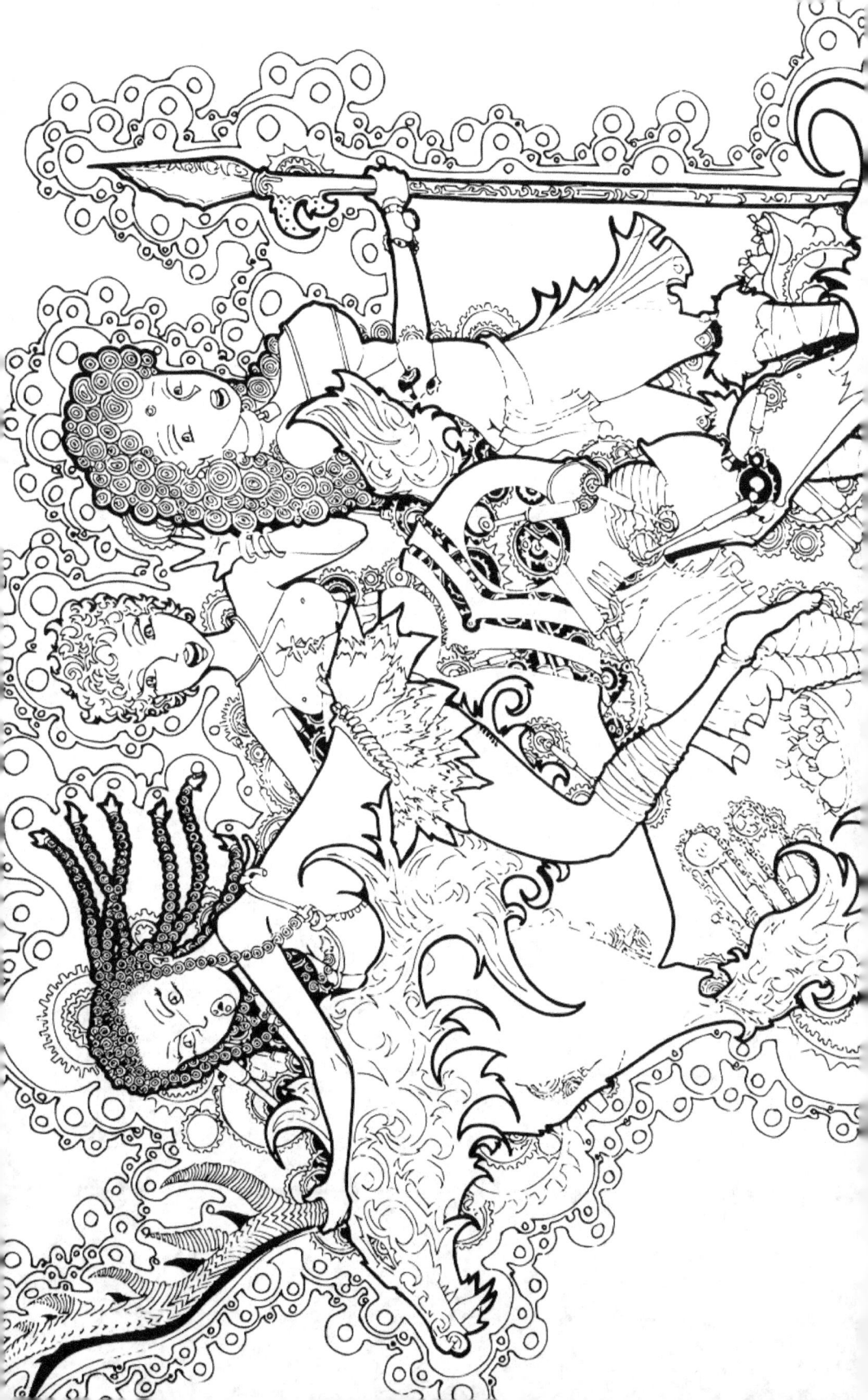

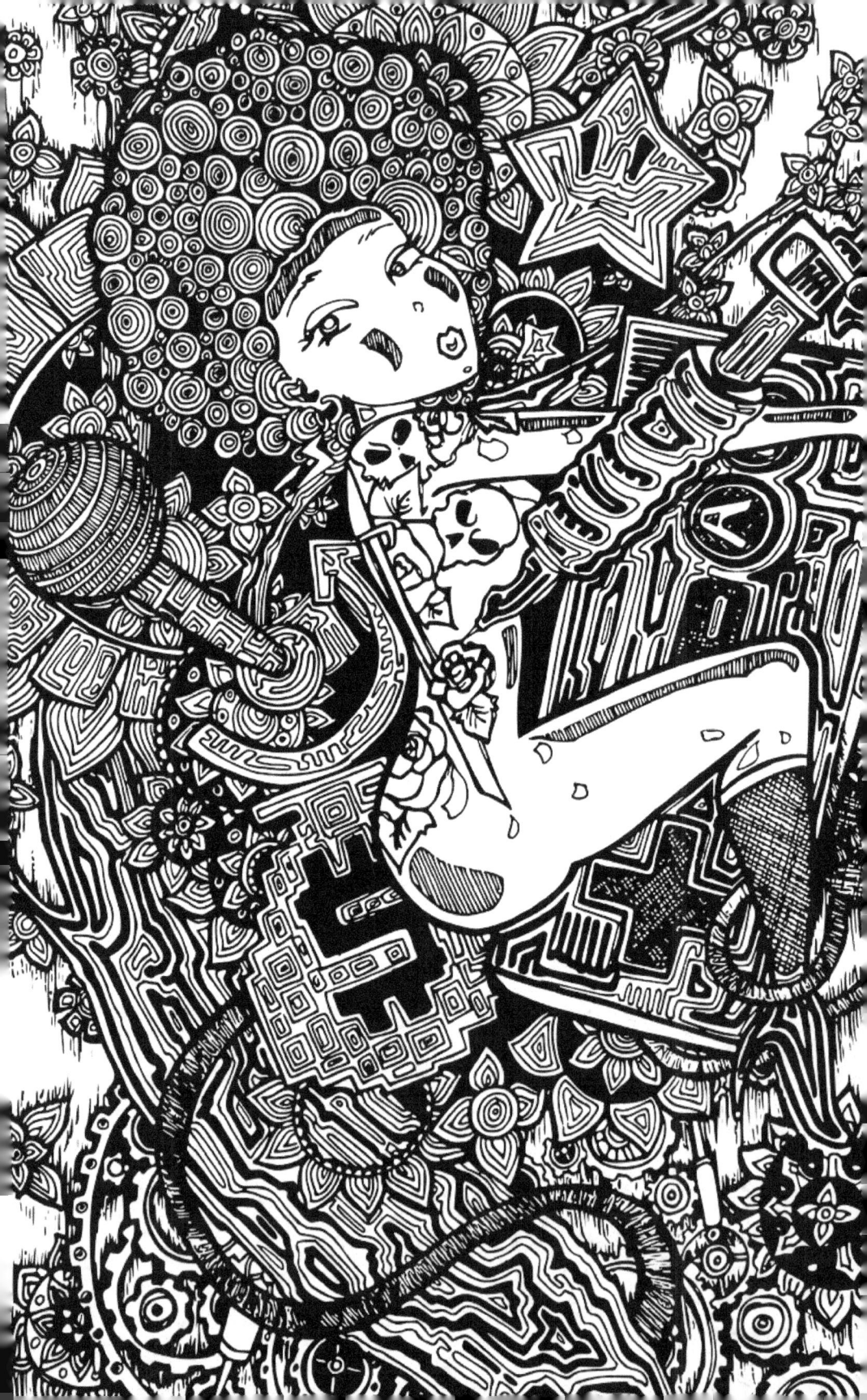

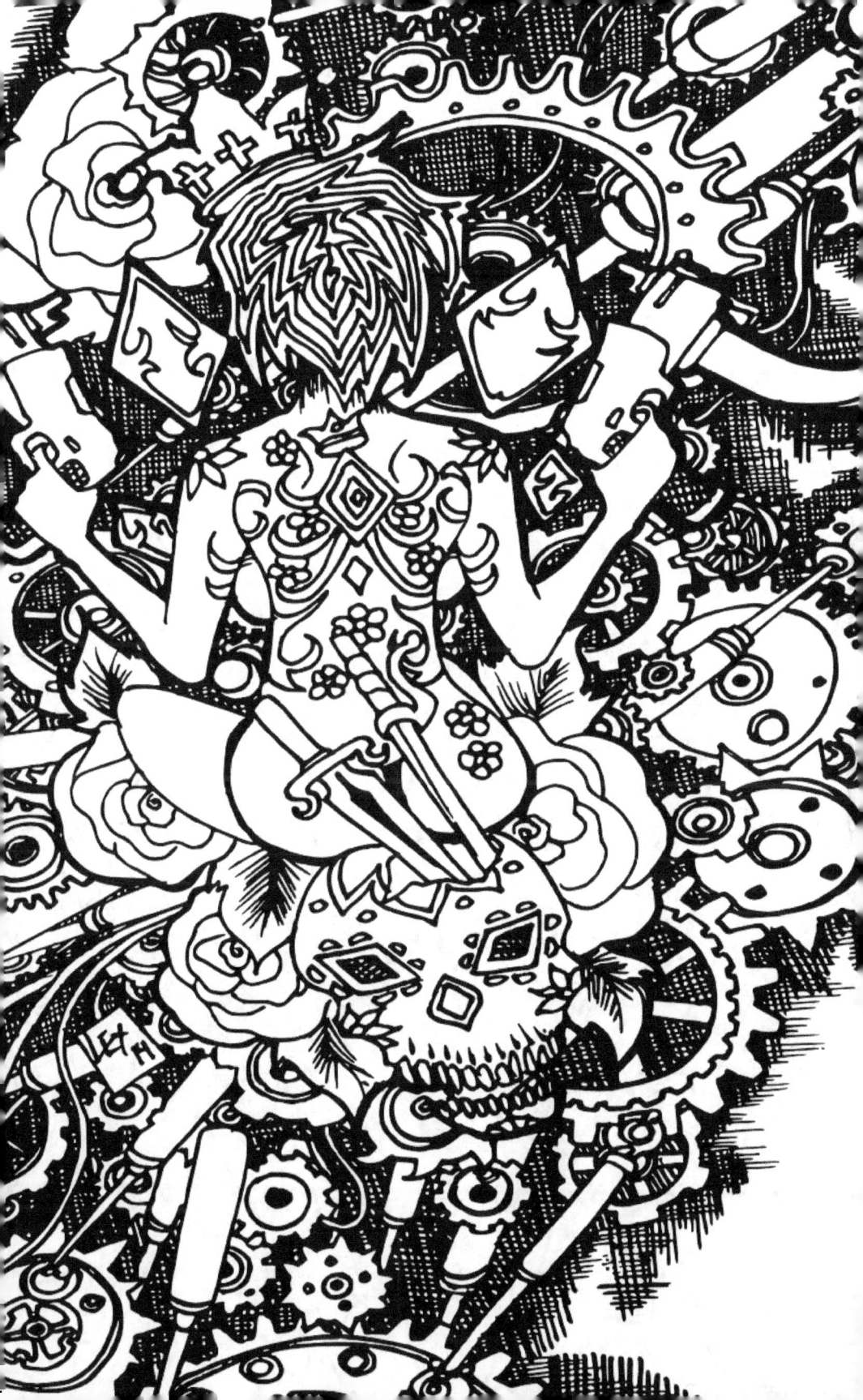

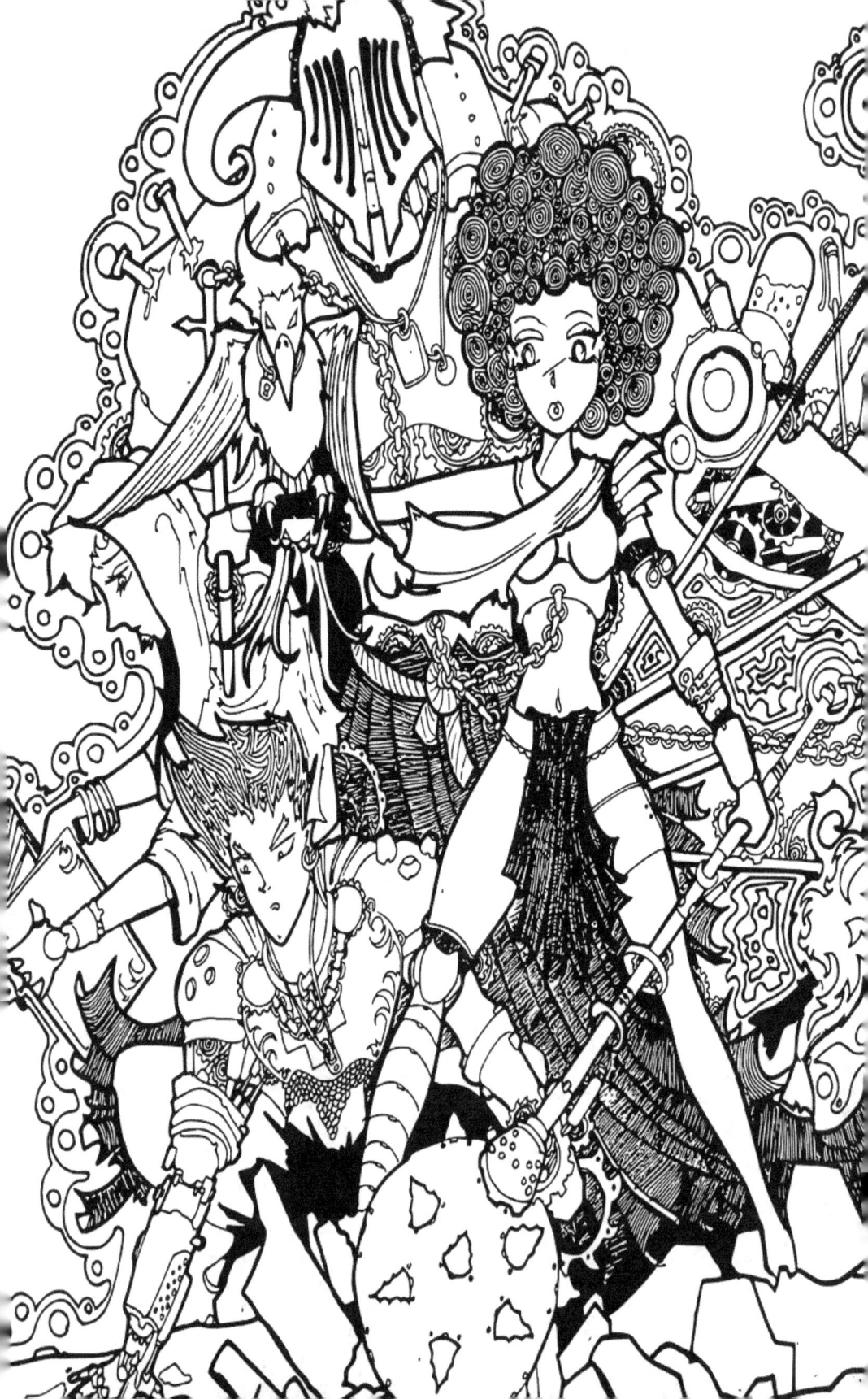

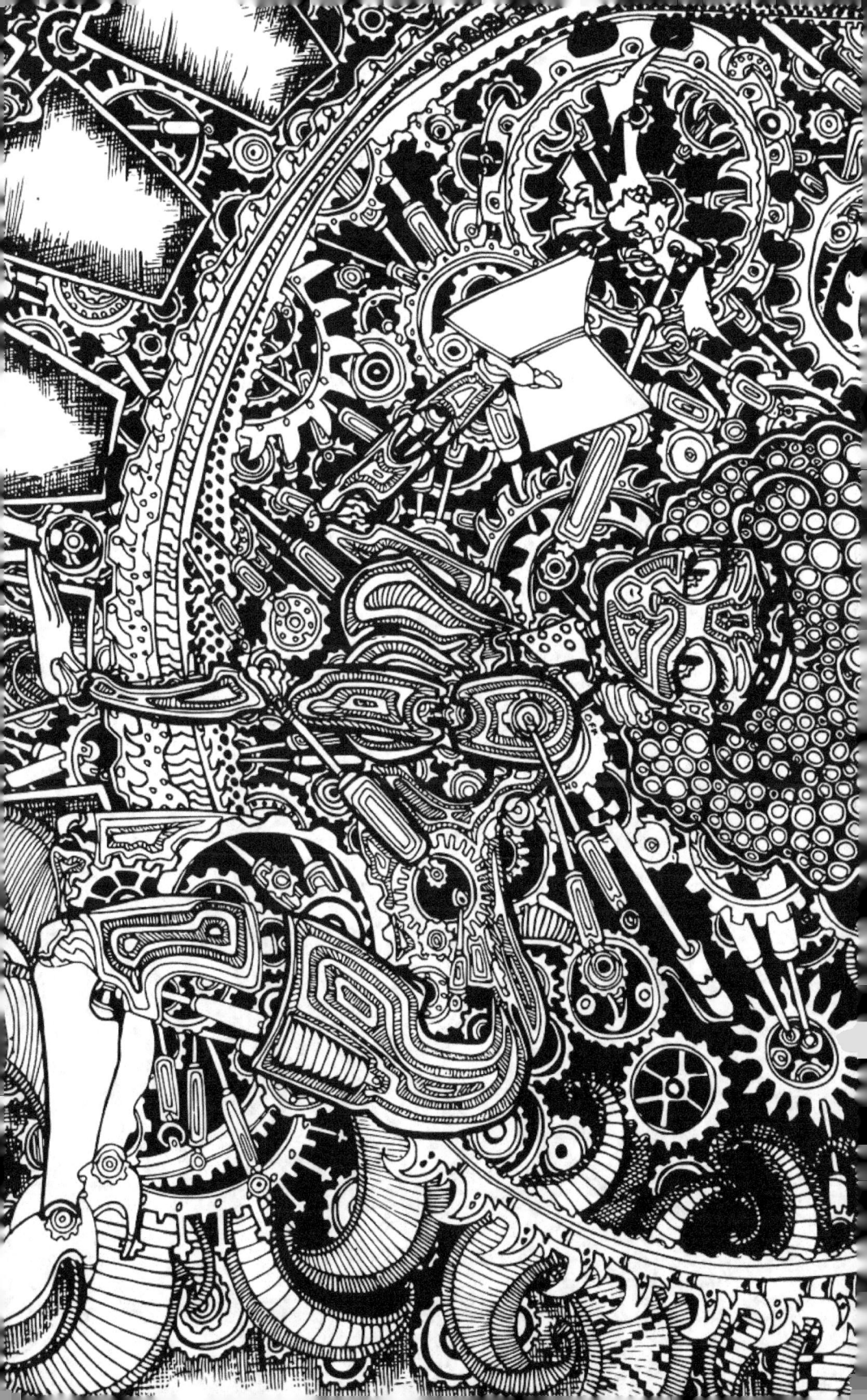

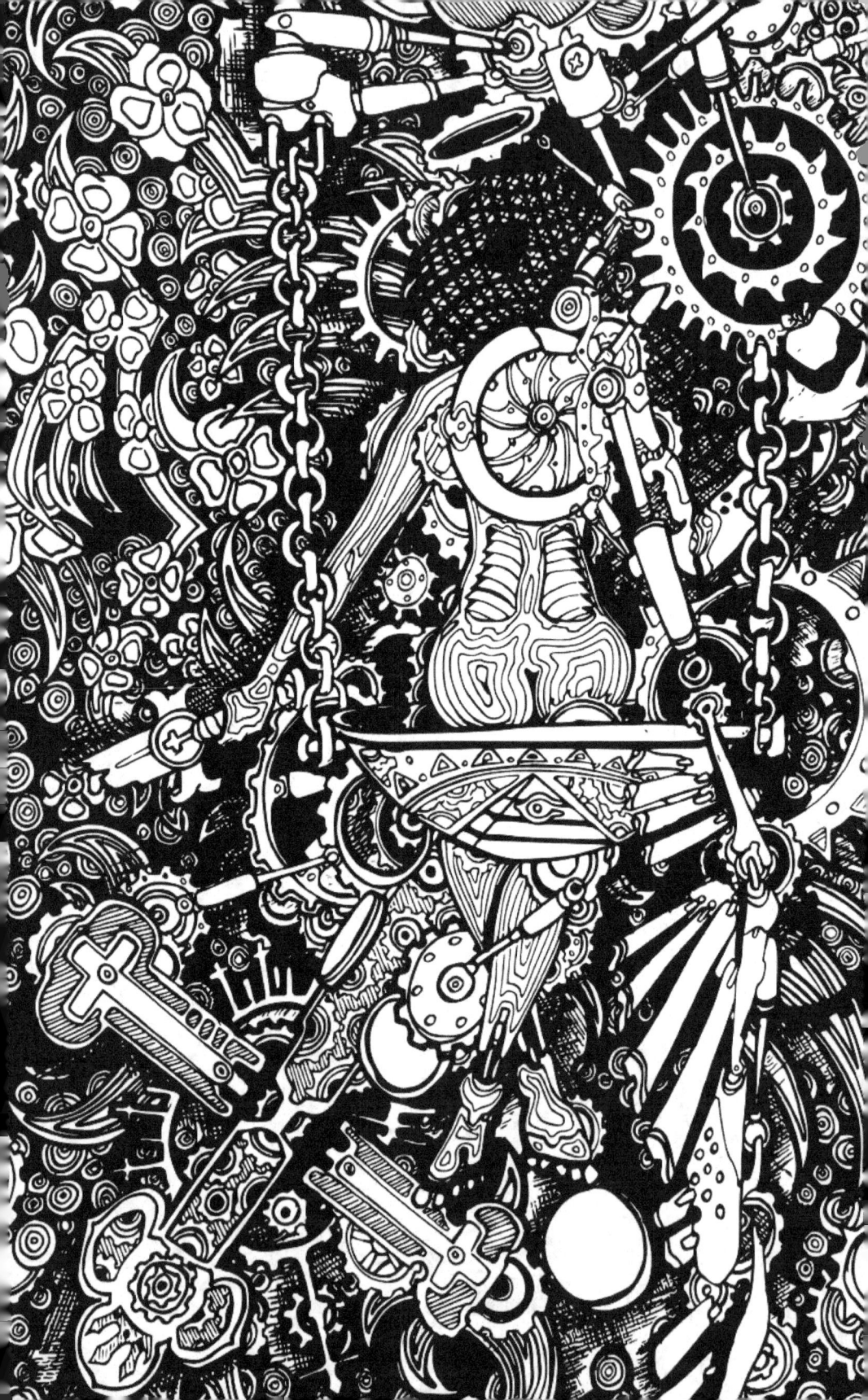

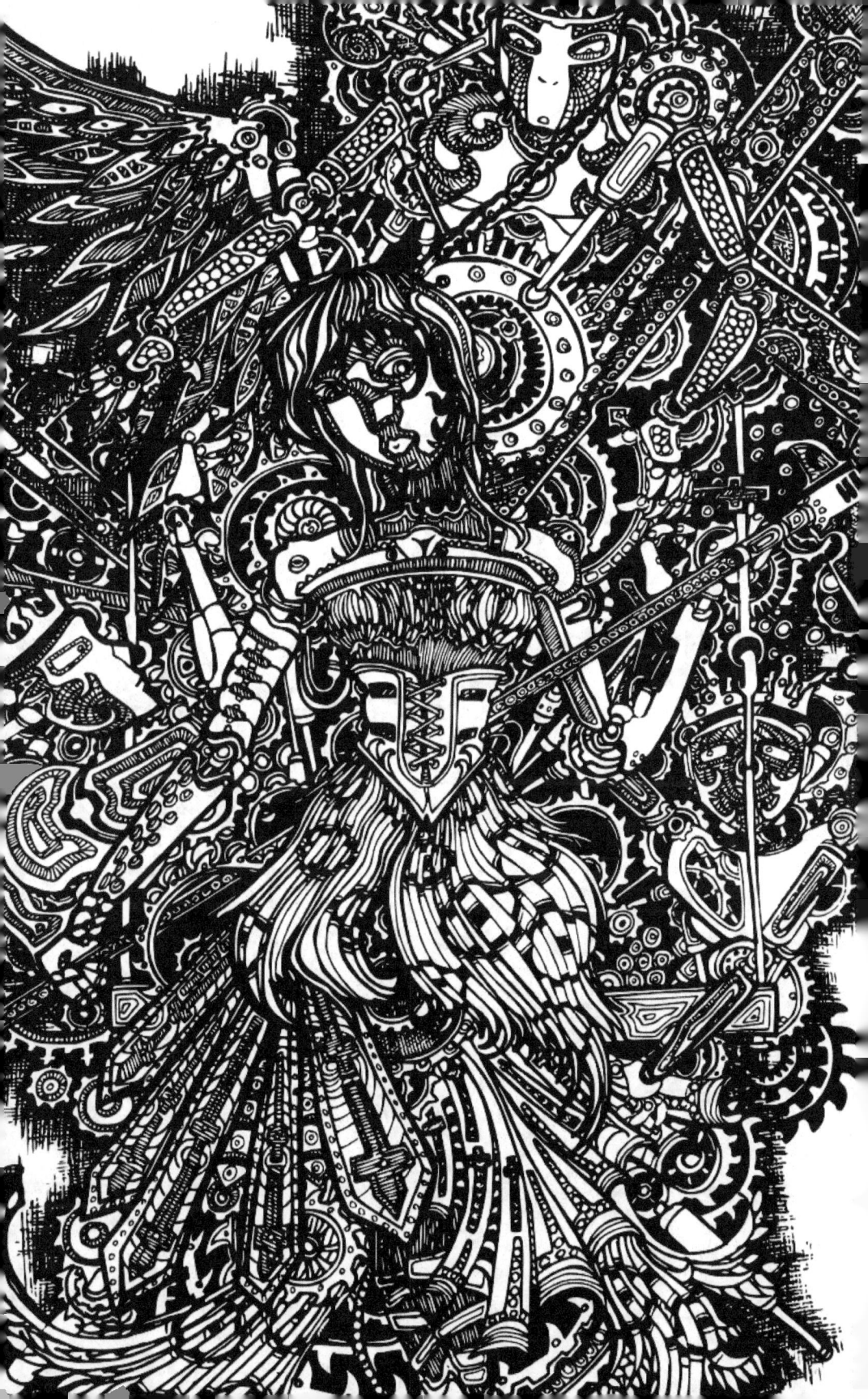

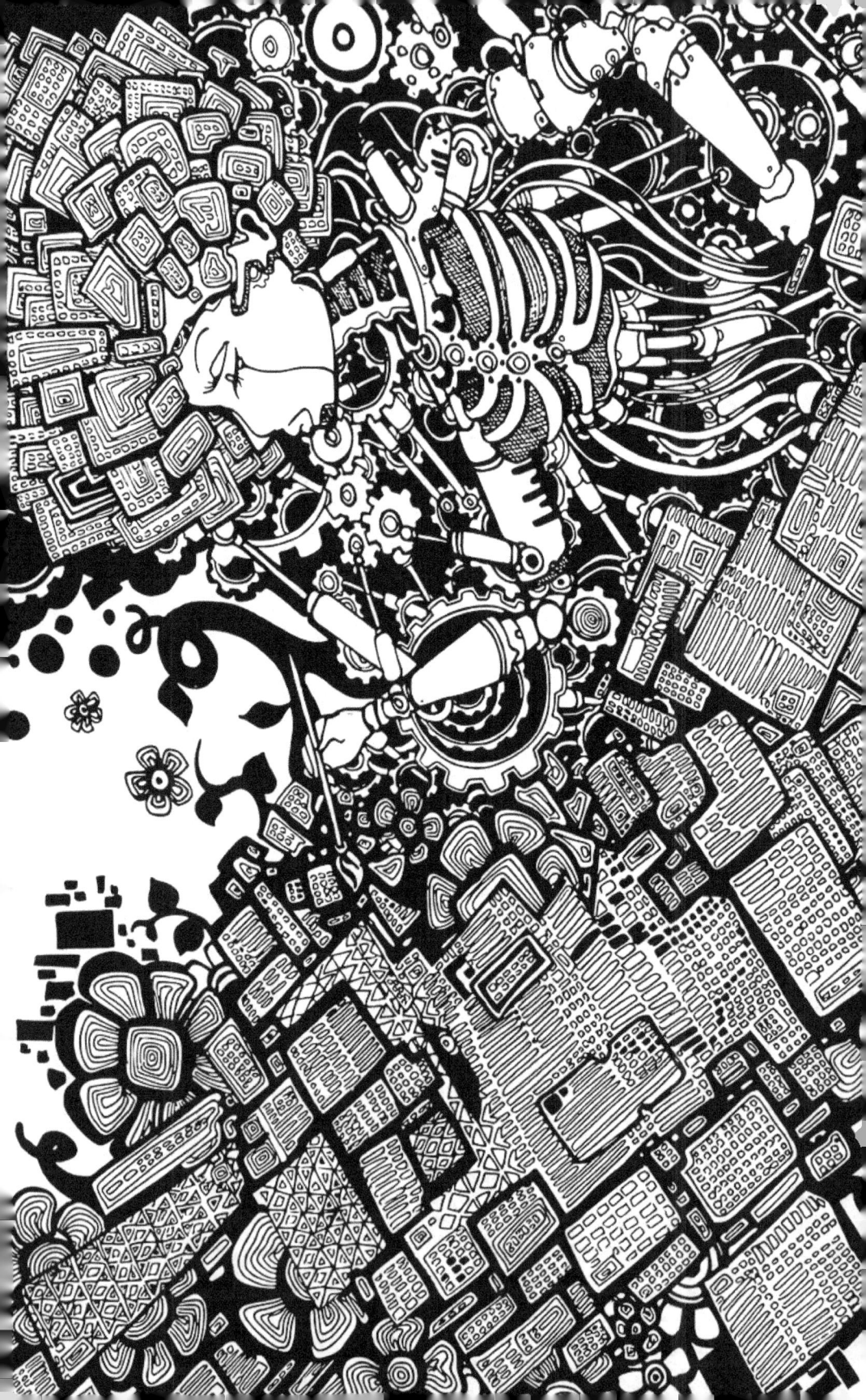

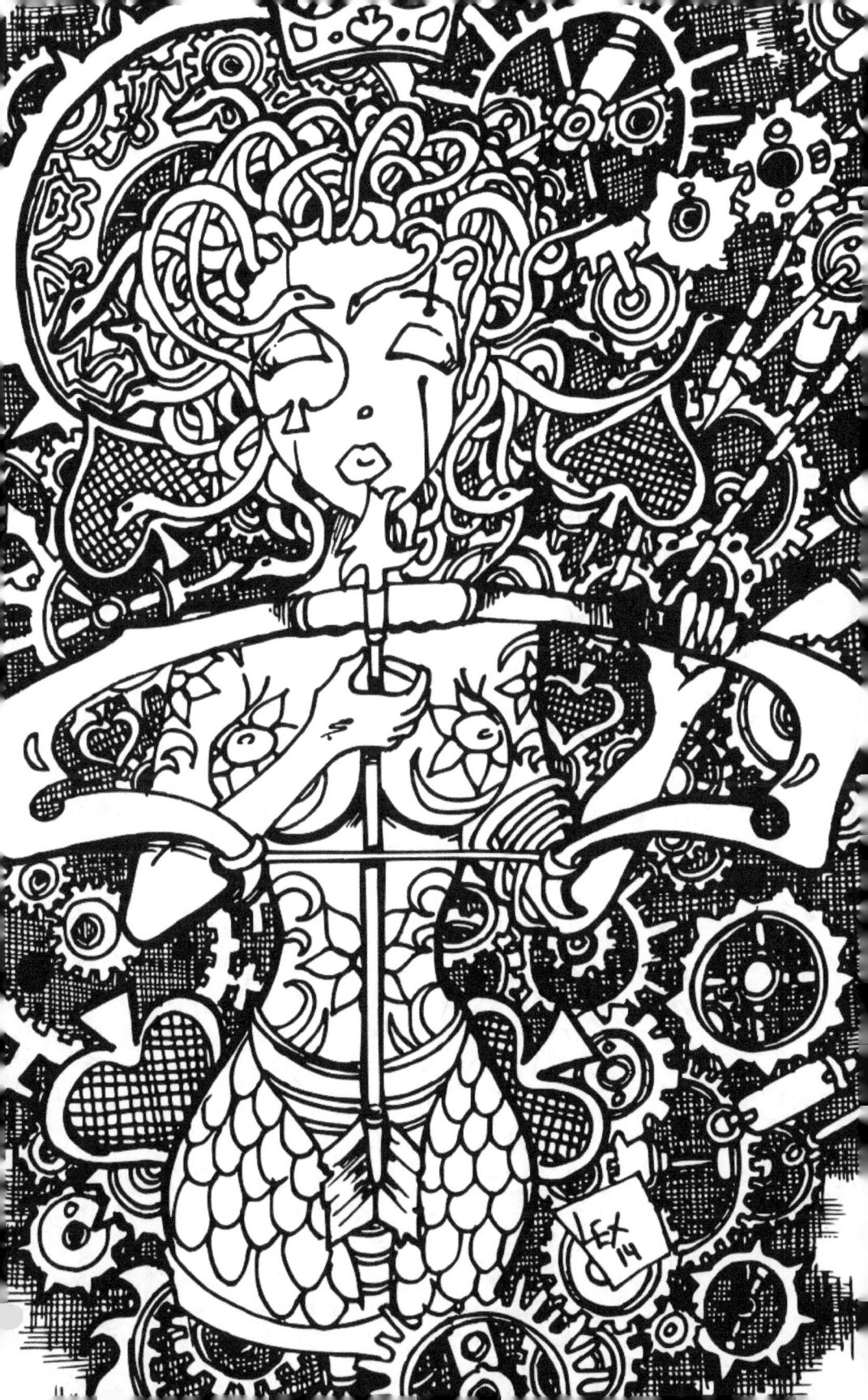

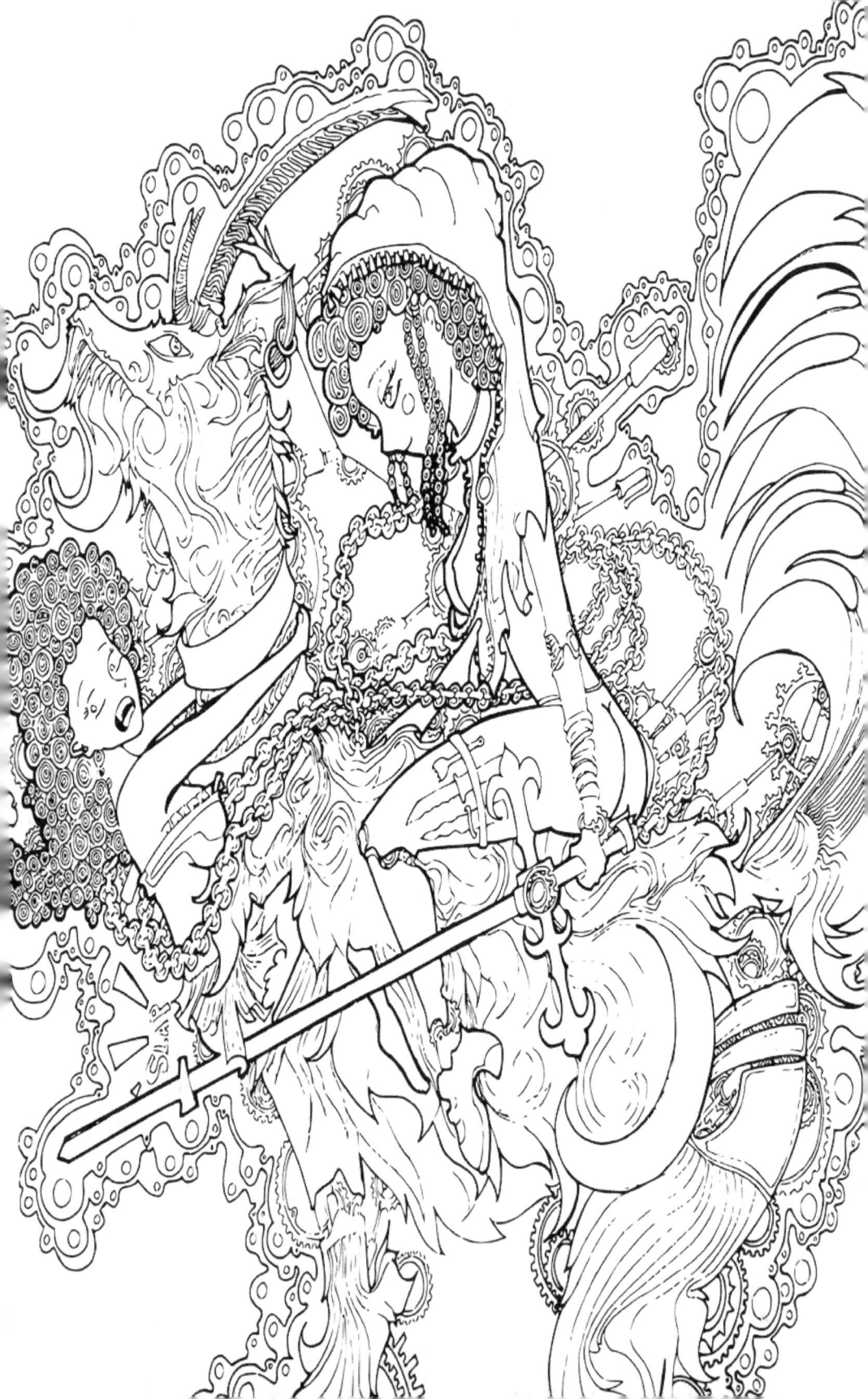

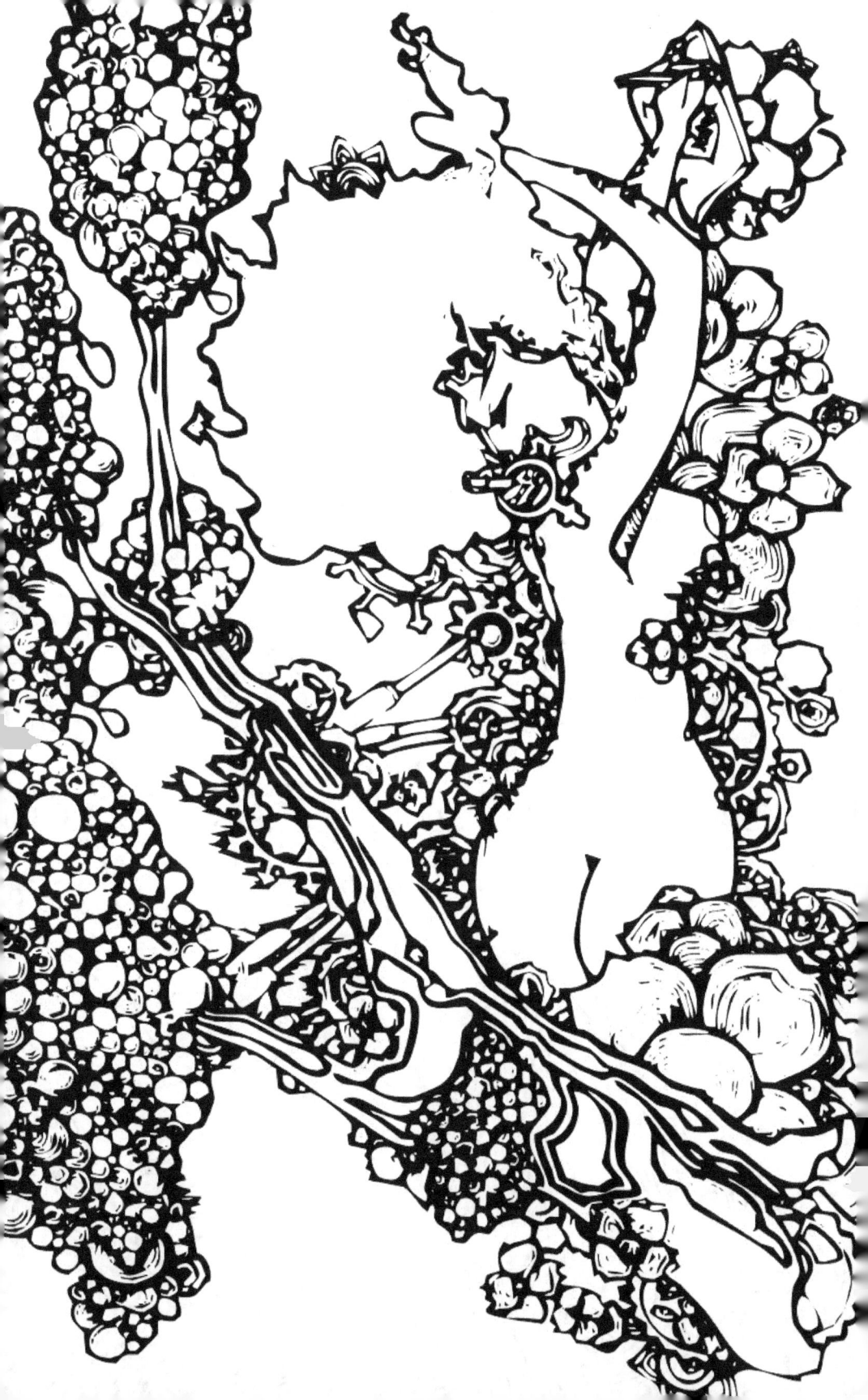

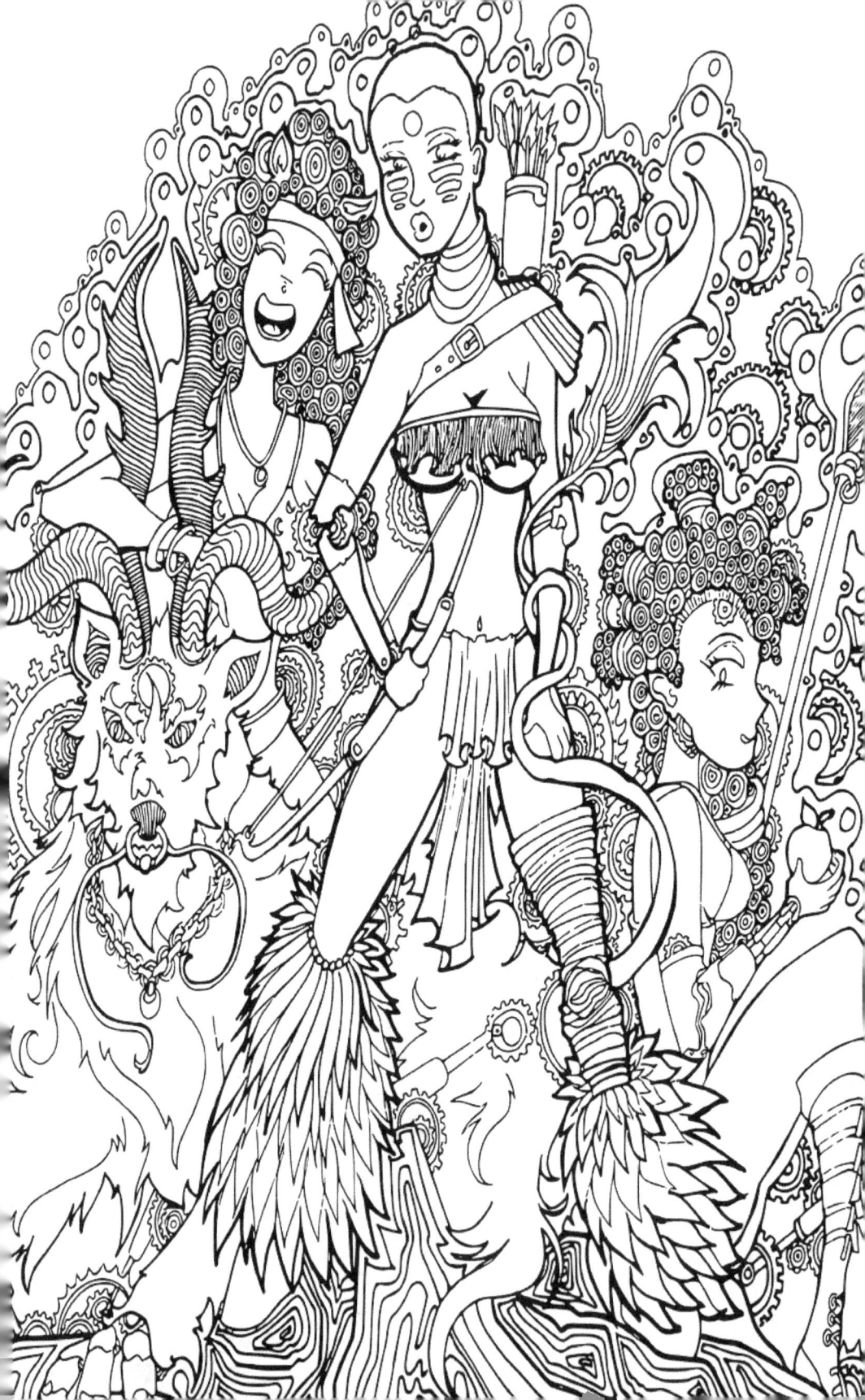